THE GOLDEN THREAD

Amali Gunasekera was born and grew up in Sri Lanka. She works in the field of Archetypal Psychology. After living in Mozambique, Kenya and India, she is now based in Cumbria. Her first collection, *Lotus Gatherers*, was published by Bloodaxe in 2016 (under her former name of Rodrigo). She was selected for Arts Council England's project *Breaking Ground: Celebrating the Best British Writers of Colour* in 2017. Her second collection, *The Golden Thread*, was published by Bloodaxe in 2022.

AMALI GUNASEKERA

The Golden Thread

BLOODAXE BOOKS

ISBN: 978 1 78037 598 4

First published 2022 by
Bloodaxe Books Ltd,
Eastburn,
South Park,
Hexham,
Northumberland NE46 1BS

www.bloodaxebooks.com
For further information about Bloodaxe titles
please visit our website and join our mailing list
or write to the above address for a catalogue.

Supported using public funding by
**ARTS COUNCIL
ENGLAND**

Cover design: Neil Astley & Pamela Robertson-Pearce.

Printed in Great Britain by Bell & Bain Limited, Glasgow, Scotland, on
acid-free paper sourced from mills with FSC chain of custody certification.

ACKNOWLEDGEMENTS

The Golden Thread was written between two places, Scotland, and Cumbria, during a period of deliberate silence I like to think of as my 'Walden Pond' years. We don't often get the space and time to experiment with different levels of consciousness, and feel our own presence profoundly; Curwen Woods was the tranquil oasis that made it possible, and so my heartfelt thanks go to Judy Boddy and Thomasina Sandys for their warmth and welcome there.

My thanks are also due to the Hawthornden Castle Fellowship, and Paul Farley and Matthew Caley for their editorial acumen. 'The Great Pause' was a commission by Ledbury Poetry Festival.

I dedicate the poems 'Reading James Merrill at Curwen Woods' to Judy, 'Worry Doll' to Pavlina and Pepi Morgan, and 'The Great Pause' to David Campbell. My gratitude always to Heike Benz, Cecilia Wood and Nim Jayasekera for love, friendship, and encouragement.

CONTENTS

May I not be the wilding deer in the woods longing for the heady musk hounding it everywhere oblivious of the flood at its own navel

I

What ails thee?

THE GRAIL LEGEND

Here, there are no clocks but a sundial
and a late-rising cockerel.

Art cures affliction he says. The low roar of the motorway arrives over the hill like life insisting on continuing, or the ocean inside a conch shell. Judy drives up through the park and lets Thistledown out—I love the way she walks her dog in the car. Through a milky film of fog, the rear red lights recede with all my troubled thought. Drizzle's slendered the lab's onyx pelt to a racing hound. He shines in damp-filtered light as if there ought to be more room for splendour in our minds.

She tells me how she walks Tottie the tortoise in the kitchen sink when her daughter is away. The image of Judy at the sink is at the back of everything, like a page beneath print. It runs together with the black swan, the broken bowl, Greece. They run and stagnate, the mind toggles. Refreshes. Toggles again.

Tottie walks in the kitchen sink. A month before Lonesome George died aged 102, being the last of his species in the Galápagos islands, I took a photo with him. I was kneeling as if he were a side-table I had lost something precious beneath, and just had a glimpse of it. Sometime later I dived off a boat and swam for what felt like eons in blue silence with a sea turtle. Its slow rowing. My marvelling. Its inscrutable expression, bored with the quotidian crossing of a deep element. Charon might have had this look, for what is one shimmering soul among a collective? Or Tithonus, for what is life without end—

It's almost Christmas. Once they believed all the swans in the world were white. A robin flits in and out of the twiggy cherry tree, a light, visible syllable of thought below the window. A little grove of gunshots from the woods behind. Deer blink across the park in a speechless gaze. Tottie walks in the kitchen sink possessing the world like a frozen delicacy. Tottie has endurance.

When the lights go down and the Maestro lifts his wand, the unfailing sea change starts within us. Against an ever-altering sky like the back of god's mind is the straightest cedar tree I have ever seen. It's way taller than the house. At the falling light there are no bravos but peacocks that cowered all day in a doorway in the yard now rising like praise, flitting among its high arches. All the people we've loved are like high praises small enough to be palm-cupped like a snow-globe. They are all there, tiny black swans on a frozen lake beyond the mapped world. The day is one long moment as if there were some great consensus in the universe and it's all happening unbeknown to me.

The castle with its pointed hat and robe of patchwork windows leans against a high cliff like a handcrafted *muñeca quitapena* abandoned by a child, its magic done. In it there's a room, a library, that is a suspended half-hexagon. Beyond the three-sided windows, the deep valley is an inflow vortex. There, fragmented and whole, the river's great untangling is heard but unseen.

A hexagon's fractions have names and precise relative measurements; one half is a trapezoid, one third a rhombus, one sixth a triangle. I place an hourglass I saw in Edinburgh [but did not buy] on the long wooden table, and beside it, the anxiety I felt when I turned the glass and set the sand to run. The setting sun shuffles on thin knees on the floor.

A feeling exists without the object—one ampoule draining its energy into the other, then reciprocating the loss and receiving endlessly. It would exist even if I had not given it a name, but you know what I mean because I gave it a name, and now for the rest of your reading, anxiety's contours shall be particular to you alone.

Still, I will tell you how I no longer require the object I desperately wanted to possess, as you will never need this poem. The idea of *object* is now a fallen leaf and unidentifiable among a multitude in a dusk-dark lane. Countless people have walked past the hourglass without ever noticing it. Others may have placed it back among the bric-à-brac because the price was not right. I did not buy it because I was rehearsing travelling light.

I turn the feeling over and over to sense its galloping
angles. It is absolute perfection, for how can a thing
that renews itself so wholeheartedly not be perfect?
Do you see the shape *you* made up until this moment

.

as an hourglass is two triangles balancing on an
infinitesimally small point?

The first hourglasses were two separate ampoules with a cord waxed in place at their union to let sand flow between them. It was later found that perfect flow could not be attained without an exact ratio; the diameter of the granule to the width of the throat needed to be ½ or more, but never greater than ½ the size of the throat.

Despite the tyranny of measurement, everything's chance if you break it down small enough, or is it a programme on infinite loop that needs an external intervention? See how each meeting is unrepeatable, but having identified through the foliage a path because of the silver tumble of a dog, I now wait every day for someone to pass by. Between what is possible and the *why* of the yearned for, there is a long and desolate road. Though some reasons are never unearthed, the heart goes on disbelieving and trusting the marvellous.

But *Ampoule* has the beauty of brimfulness of a book, or a woman about to give birth. My friend Pavli shall give birth any day now. I have not seen her since her fifth month, today she is the upflow in my heart. The birth will be induced she texts me. What need is there for a god when we do not have to rely on chance. Nevertheless, it doesn't hurt to have god on your side. I only mean something vaster than us, so we are what's falling softly filling its void. May we always know the things we carry into it.

Mother believes I will roam from sorrow to sorrow in the endless tracts of samsara because I refuse to renounce the exquisiteness of this perishable world. *Colours are the most essential qualities of a thing not lines* writes Miłosz. He's thinking of Cézanne. Having puzzled over the demarcations of colour, I see lines are fences that keep each one safe yet imprisoned within. Does *I*, being the first person suffer the same fate, hemmed in by a narrative from life's unspooling mystery? Isn't the greatest terror of the heart like the golden tiger that's caged by the freedom it senses in the spaces between bars?

Yes, there have been comings and goings; the burning tunic of the body, distant music. But none have moved your heart just so, to this exact pitch. *I am* not *my beloved's my beloved is* not *mine*. One day when all the divisions of your heart have given themselves up, you sit suffused in jewel-filtered light beneath a rose window and finally know love, love that comes too late perhaps for this dwelt world, when love with all its tenses has wandered in circles, when all the impostors are gone. Perhaps the most austere practice is not the relinquishment of the *sins* of the senses but a necessary forfeiture to know the true essence of the Beloved.

Then *You* is like earthrise, distant enough to see clearly and staggeringly beautiful. Not a state of enchantment but recognition. Like the moment I catch myself in the mirror and, for the first time do not flinch. *Catch us the foxes, the little foxes that spoil the vines, for our vines have tender grapes.* When we say *you are loved*, how often do we mean I see you? Jacob, waking, believed god was in the place the dream was dreamt and erected a visible monument. My palm shall never graze the temple of your body Beloved, but I feel the rough stubble of hair in new cut grass. As the ocean accepts rivers or rain, each of us accepts love differently, and sometimes we are unable to receive being too full of terror of the thing asking to enter us.

Buddha believed prayers were wasted wishes—there was no Beloved listening for a human voice. But if reality rests on the invisible scaffolding of our senses, could we too not be all colour? Prayer alters nothing in the world, but I am changed. Then where would I place my devotion? Timidly I unclothe my heart, separate the *I* within the *I*, watch how they concertina. Must I have one voice? You who have listened in silence, would you hear me if I gave breath to all the songs within me? Would I hear yours?

—beloved who gave the first of my beginnings, you can never know the lineaments of my hunger to experience all of this given life, *may you be spared* is her unuttered wish as I set out alone on a far journey she could not map or follow; I remember the small craft that contained and brought me to this day, I remember the child no more than six or seven with a wooden clothes horse laid flat on parquet, crouching in the improvised galleon, in carpentry never meant for seaworthiness—

But faith *is* the child with a fortune of tropes. Something stirred in the wood and gave way to ocean. Something nestled in the mind and leapt into freedom. There's always the thing beneath a desire, asking to be seen. And this dawn when I walk stiffly at the edge of the ocean, that roar too is differently heard. Beloved, it is what becomes of *I* when I am next to *You*.

Sorrow, so full of possibilities that never quite took shape, like a wanderer's shelter, find me, as *You* and *I* separately walk as if on delicate scent-trails of musk, walk through the last village into the interior, for how else shall I remember that *I am my Beloved's my Beloved is mine.*

Variation on the Fact of Spring:
One for Sorrow Two for Joy

WINTER

—and each day is a crossing of a ramshackle foot-
bridge. The world happens, skeletal against a bleaker
sky, grows unchartable encountered by the lone self,
every tremor of a step deep-felt, as if above a river's
reckless writhing—

Helpless without the camouflage of leaves, without omens, nothing gives rest, and there they are! *One for sorrow two for joy*—then, I am maddened by the non-arrival of the two dancing illusions, at what o'clock always waiting, as if they were the cure to every parting, every grief, every hope of ever crossing to another day—when fear is precise, each time new as if having just thought of it, this image, the sole anchor to the inhabited world—

the way hunger for one thing masquerades as
something else entire—forever misdirected, oh how
we hide from our own selves trying and trying to pin
something down, anything, and don't notice the world
or months, then they come with the bewildering
suddenness of dancing illusions—of course they
disappear, and I assume their shape between an
ending and a new beginning, in the terrible middle
passage, each breath a ramshackle footbridge—

Ah, the annunciation of snowdrops! Then daffodils,
primroses all fleshing the bone as I watch. I too am
caught in walking the faintest deer tracks, like the
reclamation of neural pathways that once held peace,
and all around me the flowers are raising their dazed
faces to the calling of light as if reiterating my fly-by-
nightness. I go out I return, you are always there,
O double-masked bird like a Trickster God, your
inextinguishable light and impenetrable darkness
feathers inside me—gain a love or lose a love you
are there—in the unbearable space between *I* and
the world—in tacit agreement to a hope that says,
claim the desire, it shall make you more real—

and oh, how all my secret beliefs come bounding
out of their lairs one by one showing themselves
for the first time, sacred nevertheless for their long
familiarity—I witness all my false springs of such
faith placed upon dancing illusions—

—you contain a vital clue about myself and the two masks of loneliness when a woman's body is overwritten by words: of being erased letter by letter in unmatched couplings, or that being solitary and stripped bare of other voices is to be walled off and far from every happiness. I am maddened by your perpetual vanishing, the two dancing illusions inside a double world—

when scale and distance of everything alters how can we ever know path from turning point? But you, as if hardly needing to exist, hardly needing to be real, like a thought, come and go—we have so few words between birth and death—will I ever learn to use them wisely?

Throwing open all the windows—who is this watcher that keeps them in sight day upon day *one for sorrow, two for joy, three for a girl, four for a boy, five for silver, six for gold*, who is this watcher with the abacus eyes? *Seven for a secret never to be told, eight for a wish, nine for a kiss*—a tacit agreement between the world and who exactly? *Ten for a bird you must not miss* in this unbearable space between *I* of a year ago, and unnumbered versions from all the intervening days—or way back to the one who arrived on this earth seeming to carry nothing but light breath? All that I hold today is only borrowed from some farther shore, oh confusion of dancing illusions, your endless arrivals

into the most durable of seasons more enduring than
I—the utter beauty of what waits serene, gathering
unseen plenty, holding the future very gently in its
arms. I come at this season as if across a chasm,
holding my life like some great wounding and sacred
thing.

What winter teaches me is that stripped clean of accoutrements, it is no blind time, nor illusion. Every kernel *is* and also a quiet becoming. Every moment both duration and abyss, inexhaustible—for every branch yearning skywards, hidden roots surge deep, a double reaching to master their own existence the way I long to inhabit mine. As I hold all my past selves very gently, attentive to that earliest child, I'm gladdened by the lone arrival of the bird—like the annunciation of Ardhanarishvara—emerging from the flock of wrecked things at the feet of Shiva and Shakti in their furious dance—as the world grows dark, how clearly the glowing streak is defined as if you carried some unearthly light—

If one sets off alone, companions arrive, keep step, veer off—I am gladdened by your arrival, unharmed by departure. A sudden storm and the sky is many petalled and blooming—in its centre the spiralling descent into something unfathomable. In the distance, as if at the mouth of a threshold, a stiff wind bending ancient, majestic sycamores—how easy their flex, fronting the harsh directive and I'm in mind of stories that warn of descents or turning back—Orpheus, Lot's wife [why is she nameless?] —but there are two kinds of backward glances— the one filled with regret, umbilical and terrified of rupture, perilous as a pillar of salt or dust—the other, the calm, still eye at the centre of the turning wheel at each turn chanting *how did I become who shall I become*—

the world is moulting—all summer I've lived barely
hearing for the distraction of seeing—they come they
go between what I mean to say and what is said—
they come and go where time is not sequences but
spirals of leaf-fall, never in the same place twice,
though I may look upon the same scene, I live things
over and over only in their difference. I am startled
by my proximity to every other thing and there!
one day finally, loneliness altered to spaciousness,
miraculous as my brief interlude here—there's
nothing to wait for—

II

The phoenix mourns by shaping, weighing, testing,
hollowing, plugging and carrying towards the light.

ANNE CARSON
Nox (2010)

from Nine [Miscarried] Methods

To be shallow and insufficient is perverse; to be deep and
go too far is malicious.

THE WONDROUS DISCOURSE OF SU NÜ

DRAGON FLYING

As a dragon roused from hibernation,
mounting to the clouds—is the way the ancients
ask us to encounter one another—

yet, what can we make of this doppelgänger
so removed from the damp-faced woman
learning to think in the first-person-plural
thumbing wedding planners at Waterstones,
and a shelf and twenty years apart another,
with the eternally icy fingertips weighing prospects
in self-help psychology? What can we make of—

tap the jade stalk on the mysterious feminine, carry out
the method for eight deep and six shallow—

as if being human is a long-forgetting,
having to endlessly re-teach
the body, the heart's instinct—

MONKEY ATTACK

How could there be pleasures much keener
than this—*jade hammer tapping the yin door, nine*

shallow and five deep? Him receiving her
flood, gathering all her spirit, yet like a heavy

sluice falling to withholds his; they say it
too is resurrection—for the *hundred ills* to vanish

in his being, for hunger to be banished in hers.
Split apart to their own separate selves,

they may wonder if there is one given way,
if sometimes receiving is in renunciation.

How to negotiate the wrong thing becoming
the right thing, how to know when and how

or how much—as when the monkey clings unsteadily
to a branch to pluck the highest succulent fruit,

yet withholds from its nourishment,
because he is too full of possessing it.

CLINGING CICADA

This union, that feels more like abandonment—
as when a gold flame fused to the branch
is rapt on consuming the thing it brightens

the jade sceptre knocks at her red pearl
seven deep and eight shallow until the red ball
opens wide in her and the clear call in her voice

is a kaon; the heart of the burning
turning molten while the skin is already ashening—
as when a body opens in sex without love

yet somewhere in it, the unheard elegy of love
without sex, that prize the cicada conceals
within, and is unable to spew forth.

TURTLE RISING

Among the barnacle, crab, sea anemone, she is stormless
on her back, legs up past her breasts and open
to receive some vast intimacy,
when up from the deep graveyard of lost anchors,
the turtle [the emperor of shallows and depths] comes
with his sudden retracting, sudden extending
like loving her and hating her a little for it,
like homing in for all the wrong reasons,
like aftersight and foresight emerging long after
the puzzlement of now.

Look, in the corner, the coracle of the shell;
the shelter from which one could not emerge
and confess to the beloved, 'I too am this'—perhaps
something profound or superficial, corrupt
or beautiful. Now, some fury has unleashed far out at sea,
and the shell has washed up like a truce
that's arrived too late,
long after the sanctuary emptied little by little
from the whole. What remains is a circle, a kingdom
dragged in mud with a short stubby tail,
as if drawn in a childish hand.

PHOENIX SOARING

Something is ripe for shaping. *Nine shallow and eight deep.*
Two bodies of different substance made a home
in conflagration. Let's forget the poetry of it—
of the phoenix beating its wings undefeated—
it sways, but cannot rise. How can it, in a primal forest
rancid with smoke? Its blind instinct is yellow-eyed and

reptilian. There's no decorum of departure, the heart's fruit dying
on the vine—soon kindling, the vexed feathered mind soaring.

RABBIT LICKING

The moon grabs the sea like a cloak
drags it behind,

the night returns blind to the house.

Lift up, lift up she can speak here.
She doesn't have to be picturesque and silent—

improv and frolic; the joy
of a jade rabbit leaping on the lee

of his body, appearing, disappearing
capricious but still, a kind of merry friendship,

friendship—not *a kind of* choice—
a habit, at first, undamaged, then a form of faith,

finally, all we have is its skim, long overdue—
all you can muster in a chastened or bolting

heart is friendship that hangs on
for dear life.

Stand and brush each other off. Look
the moon and the rabbit—still there.

They keep the last-ditch world safe.
And not grudgingly.

FISHES NIBBLING

A story depends on the one who narrates it.
Here's what it's like when the remedy

for *consuming the pure* and *exorcising the coarse* is;
two feminine gates pressed together,

their mouths wide open like a fish
nibbling duckweed, he, dipping

above and below as he pleases, until the red
tide rises, until all three are transfigured

in another pattern. But see how she vanishes
flowering and unflowering, singular, intimate

and unidentifiable—then, is she one or two?
—by day, Madonna, the nightly whore whose prayer

has something to do with shame.

III

Now I am ready to tell how bodies are changed
Into different bodies

TED HUGHES

Tales from Ovid (1997)

Something there, above the range of human hearing,
yet, at the threshold of perception as if enclosed in
glass, this great unceasing loom. How meticulous the
weaving of wholeness, every note so loosely held,
without fixity, without possession.

Two voices. If hearing is ungovernable, deep listening is the tuning fork conducting the pure tone of each of their nobody-but-yourself-ness. Two voices, like the suffering of being two natures, or two kindred souls past long wandering, finally come to face each other, one, bewildered; *why have you arrived here stranger, what of yourself do you recognise in me?* The other replying, *will you speak to me, just speak in the many voices of the beloved?*

Once again, a day of rain like the score to a waking dream. Two voices as the distance between the unspoken and the utterance, in slow awakening to something entwined and mutual. Transfiguration as perception looking for articulation. As aliveness searching for a body to inhabit. As joy, simple, frictionless, without the dissonance of a contradictory heart.

Not a singular *I*, that bewildered narrator divining
with their half-heart's rudimentary instrument, but a
meticulous weaving, every note so loosely held, every
question an answer, every ascent a descent, arrival
a departure, always retuning to a mediant note and
finding us asleep in our hiding places. Still, just as
inverting the triad does not change the root note, a
singular question each of us keep arriving at all our
lives, the two voices too keep arriving at *I* like a
simple plea.

A day of rain is the score to a waking dream that says
knowing the way to yield is strength—*at one point in
your life something will happen to humble you.* Glass
coming down, bead by crystal bead, the fracture of a
boundary finally revealing the element we lived in, its
shattering, no savage offering as when every grieving
is gone, the quiet expectancy for the world to re-shape
itself again, and it does, all the fallen fragments
rising through the rain, a deep commitment far
down in the mind of two voices to become a single
movement, then, though habituated thought expects
a dénouement, the sense of an ending is misleading
—they coil up again as one, like kundalini rising,
the whole of existence in gentle vibration, the glass
universe that melted and came down, rising up again
its great invisible edifice—fracture is no calamity it
is no loss, the re-shaping, not so different to love,
as when each encounter prepares you for the next
—the next enlargement of *I*, and unnoticed, each
note a keystone that fell into its rightful place.

Once again joy, how meticulous the weaving, every
note so loosely held, without fixity, without possession.
Once I called love some human form and worshipped
it until it became meaningless. Now I know love by
feel, not countenance and as an endless rising towards
articulation, as the mirror clarifies what's before it—
beyond form, in the barely traceable gap between two
notes or the reflection before it reaches the world,
love, you are there.

How meticulous the weaving, yet every note so
loosely held as if the only way left to love is by
opening the other to themselves, like kindred souls
running into each other, or second chances to feel the
future again almost here, the ripe span of its mirror
upon mirror deepening the way a phrase changes
when encountered repeatedly, a sense of anticipation,
not expectation, and joy at the encounter, simple,
frictionless, without dissonance of a contradictory
heart, In this long passage, meet me where I am
Dear X, as I have *I*, as I would you. Come sit beside
me daily at the loom.

Bend in the River

That leafy place like some defunct book of wisdom
fallen open at a random page. In it, here's the legend
that speaks in different voices. Martins loop overhead,
their flight eternal, asking *why am I, I, I? Whose story
is it anyway?*   *Soon soon* sang the wood thrush,
*love, life begins and ends in the same substance. Must
you always loop as if towards a different ending?*

Water, what strange hours you keep, carrying the past lightly, moving towards your own annihilation, you stopped dreaming of courage and leant into the fall, then, unconcerned of what fates are lining up, you go, obeying no custom no given narrative, you pass into the petty kingdom of the future ruled by that mad prince, say with a cavalier shrug *sometimes you have to do what is necessary to survive*, and slip beneath ground through the dense undergrowth of metaphors, you are at ease with awkwardness and terror, at ease with the difficult beauty of the thing just beyond sight, sensed deeply, just that much beyond grasp like a low hanging moon.

When the story becomes an alibi, you keep no ironic distance. Path and turning point, aren't they just one—the still point of a turning wheel? As you turn you say *the person I was when I arrived here isn't the person who is leaving*, you flow without being haunted by what's beneath you, the river beneath the river, and unashamed of sentiment.

You have nothing but praise for all who come to water here—Aphrodite's retinue of Erotes knee-deep in the swirling current; Anteros, Himeros, Hedylogos, Hymenois, Hermephroditus, Pathos. Nowhere else are they seen together. And there in the voluptuous trees like some pure knowing of the long experience of love, hardly visible in the shadows are Harry Harlow's baby monkeys clinging to their barren wire mothers. And ah the diviners on the banks! Bands armed with physics, microbiology, neurology and the precise and minute governance of things, as if reality was a state of equilibrium like the stretched skin of a drum, they keep pitching batons at. Yet it is strangely quiet here, though overcrowded with ghosts.

It is more the idea of the river than the river, the river saying *I am trying to get this right*. Just as at birth one learns to live in a different element, in this place an *I* is forming, it is nature's gamble and relic. Perhaps our lives are only the stories we tell ourselves. Call and response, a thatch of half-narratives. There's no dwelling place. That little house in the distance only marks a place that balances east and west, north and south, is nowhere we can return to. Here is our bewilderment of having come to the same place of worship all our lives only to find the gods have changed hands unbeknown to us.

After rain when light hits the treetops coal-tits have risen like flotsam. Look at them flickering there so tiny, so full of industriousness and joy. Since I know nothing of them, I know the joy is really my bright clutter because there's no need for a beloved to feel any of it, one merely needs a *You* to express what is already present in the heart. In the narrow place between what you dreamt of and what's possible in the world, there's another small house there, near water. Perhaps all we can say is *we can be happy there, tell me what you want.* We are new in this ancient world. Look at that far blue ridge. The human dawn too is beautiful.

Variation on the Fact of Spring

So long now since the sun looked at the earth with
desire. After a sudden storm the robin hops, a
blunt needle passing in and out of hessian mending
the earth's blue lips.

Rilke said *God is the hidden place that heals again.* As if for the first time, life comes; oh the lilacs initiated into something new, the deep rush of blood in the tulip—*you are meant for this! You are!* But too early in the season for blossoming, they die. Why so hasty, why so single-visioned?

But look, there is no bitterness at all! Pumpkins thump to the ground. Dogs lie spent, sun filters through to leave dark pawprints on grass. Cows flicker whitely behind trees. Buttercups, as if to say *what shall I place in the centre of this day*. Why this human need for eternity in one form only? Along Coniston shores trees are balancing both terror and wonder, like waiting to die on hospice beds, roots clutching thin air. How earth and air weaken each other. Martins loop overhead, non-committal. Death leaves only traces in passing through this ancient world. Oh what have you done with the small inheritance of the body? Who will mourn the senseless suicides? Why did nothing give them the comfort of knowing that beneath the ephemeral is endless duration, that repetition is only the mind's instinct. They went unable to distinguish which is the echo which is the voice.

Spring arrives like using the cause of sickness to heal the sickness. The wind rose, cherry blossoms ruptured making the grass wince with cargo. Two ducks wade through like snowbound travellers. They leave a faint trace in the whelm that mends close behind them, faint as the difference between abundance and false glamour. Between gratification and nourishment. Suddenly the green mind of the tree is visible again.

Didn't you know that beneath all the prevarication and red herrings the one thing the world is really after, is resurrection, to die again and again to find that pure place of arriving again, into becoming, oh how to learn to be so at ease with it, in the dwelling-place of joy in that turning moment. Then gone again, disguised as want, without beginning or end. Summer's stasis and stupor is no match for this.

This blossoming is like every kindness that births another, it's not beauty at all. The red balsam, not really lust-addled, not an offended goddess, but more like the day after finally firing the therapist. Even in the thistle—that awkward guest so finely attired—there's no posturing. It's not flattered by attention or thinking *how will you seduce me now?* Beauty is an austere idea, aloof, remote. Yet like the difference between art and artifice, on a high and desolate plain, wildflowers are themselves, beautiful, without need for witness.

The whole world watches the earth expectant, *do it again do it again*, the role it fills without will. Over the house dawn tigers gold and black the cedar's limbs. In the window the flicker of two long winged birds, crane-like but unidentifiable, flying in tandem like a man with a suitable wife, a sight beyond a vantage-point yet coming through innocent arrangement of conditions precisely aligned. Whatever grows, grows because of arrangement for a seed's requirement, the seed arrived unhurried, and by chance since the first fall, repeating an old truth in a new language.

Look at young love, how it requires suspended disbelief, each of them subscribing to a common narrative, and sometimes with no room to be themselves in a singularity, they bear and whittle each other, and are perplexed, yet still, mostly grateful to enter the blood sport of union not knowing the difference between gratification and nourishment.

But what does not grow dies and petrifies. Again,
the earth limbers up its stiff muscles, the dancer
that's neglected a daily routine returning to fluidity.
The whole world is built on autobiography, there's
the woman now dead-heading roses like her own
history, the man courting danger, in a moment of
innocence above the new fruit yet unreached for.

A clutch of robins, tight knit as a carpel, tinker on the gravel—at the sudden cry of a carrion crow they scatter—a many-petalled flower opening, as an inkling resolving into a feeling. Crocuses through snow, return return until the earth knows you! Make something beautiful of the harrowing, as that woman and man, all through spring wait for the overgrowth simply for a chance to prune, shape and re-shape.

And there in the distance the estuary, after long passage, radiant, resting on the chest of the one she loves. In the green world, what now, when we have arrived at the future we've wished for, *what now what now* the martins loop overhead.

The Great Pause

Spirit without moving is swifter than the mind

UPANISHADS

I must ring of silence, for the pair of goldfinches alighting on the sill do not see me, nor the robin that rootles by my feet at the lakeshore. Three fields up a green lane, tributaries of cows pour towards me from a knoll when I pause by the gate to play *Beethoven's Silence*—ah the ease after allowing the heart its truest desires! The way we witness each other sets me chuckling all day to think of it—and the absurdity of human posturings and façades. Three paced notes, the next folding down as if marking a page, a fifth to flip to what's next—Cortázar has somehow read the texture of my own perception—

Wake at no-crack-of-dawn glow. Some days the sun is flung from a drystone wall, finally loosened from years of weathering. This dying craft is everywhere. From a high cliff, they are the partitions of a maze at ground level we absently steer by. On such grey days I wonder, how did I not see the pleasure of peeling an orange before? A traced golden mean of the out-spiralling rind echoes the pale blue tinged snail shells I bring back from the fell as I walk, walk the metaphor it seems to me, of pilgrimage, as if to escape some sentence, as if my being alive depended on it, over the fell and down to the church, and back up again. Bones begin to rise to the skin through strata of earth. In an algae-filtered jade glow in the woods, I am empty and full all at once—I must have stood still so long that on turning I startle a stag— the incredible intimacy of a hovering moment of communion, then the quickening into two different entities—and I know suddenly that it is not necessary to go anywhere, where I keep arriving at is the perimeter of that metaphor with no stone altar, a limp thing so easy now to turn away from—

again and again the trail flows me—at first, through barren gullies, then solar flares of gorse like remembrances elsewhere, early purples, fat bullions of dandelion, hyacinth, multiplying like the tendency of energy to repeat the paths it once took—never remaining, they play some great game of pass-the-baton, or are they circles of prayer—next ramson, yarrow, foxglove. Oak, rowan, birch that waited like hungry ghosts becoming happy buddhas—not a thing notices me, I am no go-between, I am so light the fell lifts me up, but that first brown valley stays with me a faint overlay, like the thing I had forgotten I had forgotten, now afraid to lay it down, afraid to remember it completely, such a human predicament

—still, the fell lifts me up, the horizon of breath is endless—in the city the wind used to be white noise, here I am deep in its throat, I am the cords through which air flows to give utterance to the world—city by city, country by country the world is shutting down, the longer I go without speaking my own voice weakens but the wind moves touching everything

—all there is, is this ever-alteringness, and into it, from Argyll, David sends me the inner landscape of a magnolia campbellii cleaved in a gale. He says *modest good news in bad times, they are flowering for the first time eighteen years since planting.* It reminds me of a zen temple, a dawn-drawn stupa with a jade finial against an immaculate backdrop of a lake in mist.

I respond with a recording of a two-ply song; the first cuckoo of the season! Then, a hullabaloo above the treetops—the fierce pair climaxing a whodunit. He sends wild seas at the Atlantic edge near Jura, and an island faintly visible, it's where Orwell wrote *Nineteen Eighty-Four*, he says. From Cumbria, I send the unearthly radiance of dew, the delicacy of worlds poised on a single vaulted blade of grass like the blessings of friendship, and a thousand moons jostling on a tiny white feather—oh, how water accepts and keep accepting light! One day, a cloud of rosy Himalayan primula he rescued from a crumbling castle; progeny of Joseph Hooker's Sikkim saplings. He says, *soft rain today. Badly needed*, I send lambs scalloping hot afternoons, macros of bees, those little flame bearers. All this looking out, and when from habit I turn to my history, it's all gone—

beneath the coordinates of who I was when I
arrived here, there's been a great undoing of a
story; beginnings, middles, imaginary places my
ongingness elemental, not willed but a happening, I
am the lightest emboss on air like Ariadne's Corona
Borealis tossed on the lawn backlit by hoarfrost, or
the astonishing flight of Pegasus overhead my scrying
app makes visible—with trial and error there's Cygnus
splendid upon a rug! Or Sagitta the arrow Heracles
buried in the eagle fretting on Prometheus' liver—
someone once said *resurrection needs a body, immortality
needs a soul*—it's as if constellations hidden in plain
sight have been declaring again and again, *may you
inherit the kingdom of yourself*— all this time, where
was I lost? Who is this, rising through the strata of
earth? Who is this walking me home through twilight?

Bonsai

a tree that has
not known a bird

a tree that is
voiceless without

wind   sometimes a
man powerless

to climb the miracles
at his feet

NOTES

Worry Doll (20):

Spanish *Muñeca quitapena* is a small handmade cloth doll originating from Guatemala and refer to the legend of a Mayan princess named *Ixmucane*. They are given to children as a trusted friend they could confess worries and fears to and are also used in modern child psychiatry to act as an 'agent' between the child and adult.

Beloved (28):

Contains lines borrowed from *The Song of Songs* ('Song of Solomon') from the King James version of the Old Testament.

from **Nine [Miscarried] Methods** (48):

The Wondrous Discourse of Su Nü is a handbook of sex from the Ming period in China. The techniques of sexual alchemy (based on Douglas Wiley's translations) are attributed to the goddess Su Nü (Immaculate Woman) and take the form of answers to questions posed to her by the Yellow Emperor. Douglas Wiley says: 'The nine times refined elixir uses the dragon and tiger to play the roles of yin and yang, lead and mercury, to represent male and female.'

'Madonna–whore complex' was identified by Sigmund Freud as a form of 'psychic impotence'. He wrote: 'Where such men love they have no desire and where they desire, they cannot love.'

Variation of the Fact of Spring: One for Sorrow Two for Joy (35):

Ardhanarishvara is a composite androgynous form of the Hindu god Shiva and his consort Parvati (also known as Shakti), and is depicted as half male and half female. This image symbolises the idea of 'duality in unity'.

Spiegel im Spiegel (56):

Spiegel im Spiegel ('mirror in the mirror' referring to an infinity mirror) is a composition in the 'tin-tinnabular' style for a single piano and violin by Arvo Pärt (1978). In musicology, the 'mediant' (Latin: to be in the middle) is the third scale degree of a diatonic scale, being the note halfway between the tonic and the dominant.